"A critic at my house sees some paintings. Greatly perturbed, he asks for my drawings. My drawings? Never! They are my letters, my secrets."
~Paul Gauguin

The Art Of Man
Volume 20
Spring 2015

Editor E. Gibbons
Art Historian Grady Harp
Copy Editor Paul Rybarczyk
Layout, Design, Production E. Gibbons
Publisher Firehouse Publishing

ISBN-10: 1940290384
ISBN-13: 978-1-940290-38-6

Information: *The Art of Man* (1-20) is a quarterly journal founded in 2010, www.artofman.net, produced by www.FirehousePublications.com.
Availability: Please visit www.theartofman.net for the most current pricing, store locations, and information on both current and back issues. For questions, please e-mail LOVSART@gmail.com or call 609-298-3742. Price is subject to change without notification.
Submissions: *The Art of Man* considers submissions of artists and gallery interviews. Contact LOVSART@gmail.com, subject "AOM Submission," for additional information.
Advertising: For advertising rates, wholesale bulk pricing, and other information, LOVSART@gmail.com.
Distribution: Online through our website www.theartofman.net. For information e-mail LOVSART@gmail.com.
Printing: Volumes 1 - 20 were published quarterly by Firehouse Publishing, headquartered at 8 Walnut St., Bordentown, NJ 08505. Volumes following number 20 will be annual editions published in the late autumn of of each year, starting in 2015.

© 2015 by Firehouse Publishing and Firehouse Gallery. All rights reserved. No part of this book may be reproduced without the express consent of Firehouse Publishing, Firehouse Gallery, and its owner, E. Gibbons.

Right: Goryaev, *Archer*, pastel on cardboard with gilding, 118 x 70 cm. 2014
Cover: Furguson, *Coy*, 36 X 24 in. (Media? Year?)
Rear Cover: Ivatts, *Guantanamo, Diptych II*, mixed media, oil on canvas, 2008

CONTENTS

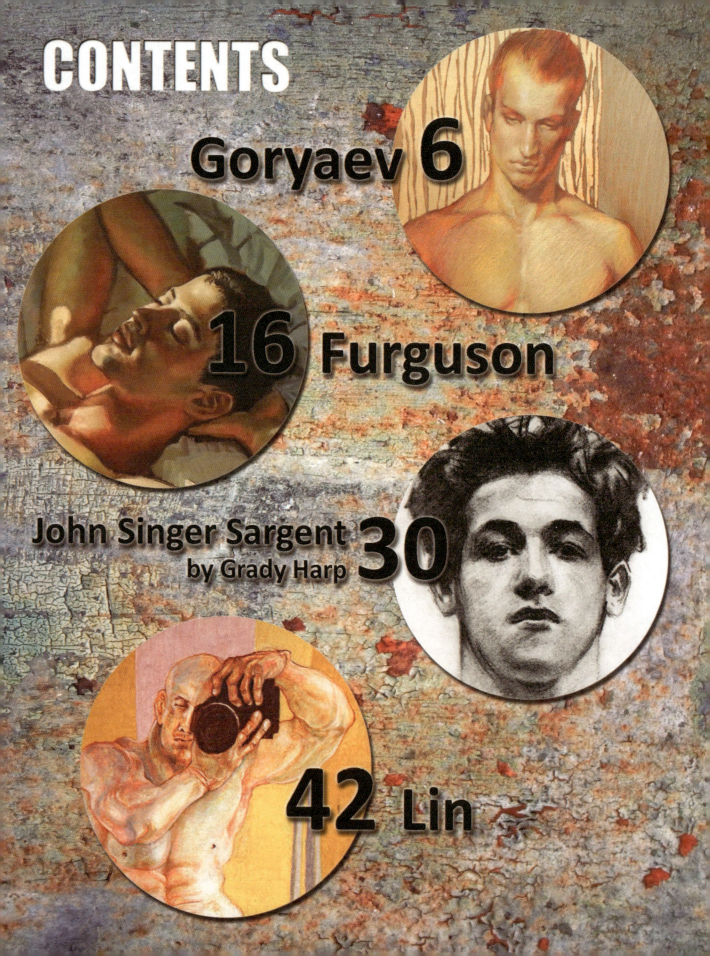

Goryaev 6

16 Furguson

John Singer Sargent 30
by Grady Harp

42 Lin

Ivatts 50

58 Kempinski

Daumont 66

77 ARTIST DIRECTORY

Viktor Goryaev

Art of Man: Please tell us a bit about yourself.
Viktor Goryaev: I was born in Ukraine, in the industrial city of Krivoy Rog, where I continue to live and create my art. As I can remember, I have always painted since childhood. As a child I loved to draw fabulous birds. At age eleven I went to art school. In 1984 I went to Krivoy Rog Pedagogical University for graphic arts. After graduation, I taught decorative arts at the same university for two years.

Now I engage in painting and I actively take part in art exhibitions in Ukraine and abroad. My works are in private collections in Ukraine, Germany, Russia, and Israel.

AOM: Why do you focus on the male figure?
V.G.: In my work I often turn to the nude male, because I think it's perfect. It has many strong expressive possibilities as a force, powerful plasticity, and expression.

AOM: What do you think makes your work so unique?
V.G.: I work in a variety of ways and techniques of painting, combining both arts and crafts. I like experimenting, using different materials and technologies. In one work, I can use many different media and methods; this is my way of working, my view of the world, is unlike the majority of artists.

Left: Goryaev, *Victorious*, oil on canvas with gilding, 110 x 70 in. 2012
Right: Goryaev, *Maritime Chimera*, proprietary media, 140 x 60 in 2003

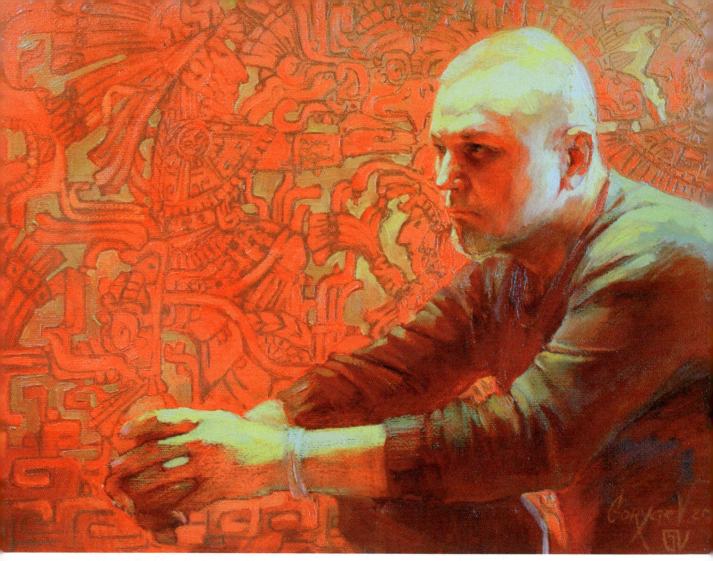

Goryaev, *Self Portrait*, oil on canvas, 45 x 60 in. 2013

AOM: What do you hope for in your future?
V.G.: Like any artist, I would like my paintings to be seen by lot of people. My art would convey the vision and understanding of all beauty. I sincerely believe "beauty will save the world!"

AOM: What influences you as an artist?
V.G.: As I mentioned, I love to try new things and it shows in my work. Recently I visited the Museum of Modern Art Peggy Guggenheim in Venice and it pushed me to new creative experiments in painting, particularly monochrome painting as seen in my works titled *Terracotta*, and *Yellow*. These and my other works can be seen on my personal website http://goryaev.com.ua,

AOM: Who would be your artistic idols?
V.G.: My idols in painting are Rembrandt, Michelangelo, Andrei Rublev, Nicolai Feshin, Mikhail Vrubel, Giovanni Boldini, Gustav Klimt. The work of these great masters had a big impact on all my work.

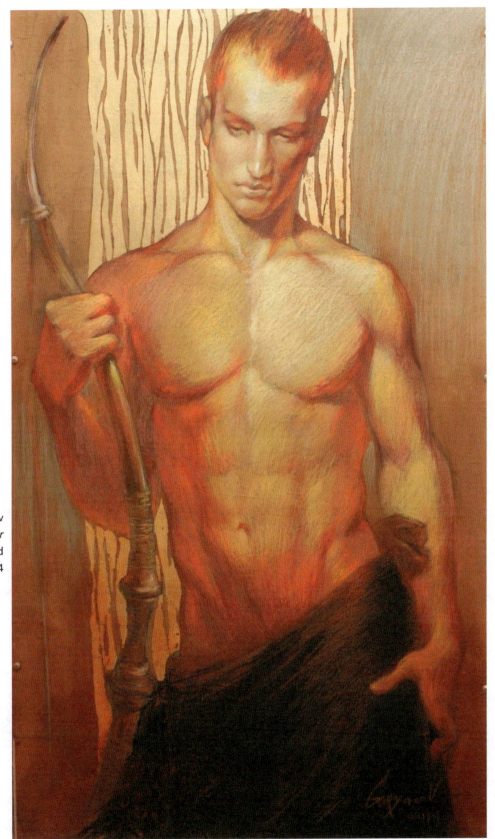

Goryaev
Archer
cardboard, oil pastel, gold
120 x 70 in. 2014

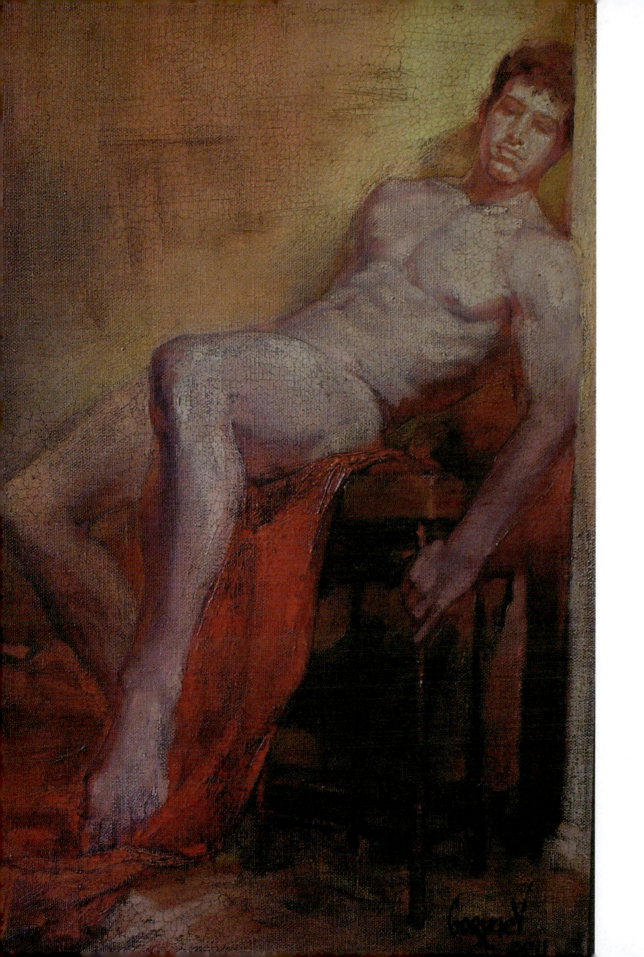

Above: Goryaev, *Dream*, oil on canvas, 80 x 45 in. 2008
Left: Goryaev, *Sleeping*, oil on canvas, 90 x 75 in. 2011

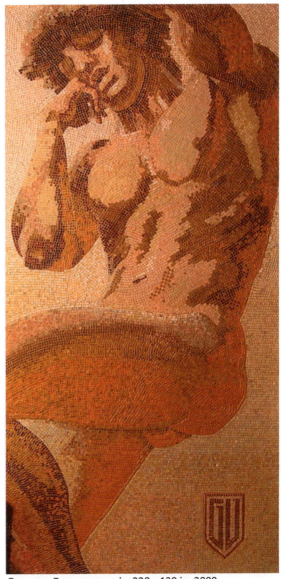

Goryaev, *Dreams*, mosaic, 220 x 120 in. 2009

AOM: Do you remember your first exhibition?
V.G.: For a long time I did not do exhibitions. My first exhibition was held in Kyiv In 2004 in the gallery of the National Union of Artists of Ukraine. It was a great success. Since that time my work has been regularly featured in different exhibitions in Ukraine and Europe, and I participated in an art auction in Leipzig Germany.

AOM: Where do you find your models?
V.G.: Models for my paintings are my friends and their friends. I would love to have David Gandhi model for me though some day. He's got everything that interests me as an artist, style, plasticity, and a strong masculinity.

Goryaev, Celtic Man, oil on canvas, 60 x 115 in. 2012

AOM: Any funny stories with a client or gallery?
V.G.: I have always had a good relationship with galleries and with customers too, although there are unusual situations. There was once a client who liked my painting, but when he knew the price, he decided to calculate the cost by calculating how much the canvas, stretcher, frame of the picture, and on how much I spent paints, etc.

In response to it I laughed and asked him, "and how much does inspiration cost?"

AOM: What do you do when sales are slow?
V.G.: I am versatile artist. When painting sales fall, I accept orders for manufacturing of leather accessories—male and female bags, belts, wallets, covers for albums and books, or I manufacture decorative items for interiors—lamps, lamp shades, vases, or decorative panels of leather and ceramic. I also develop and design leather garments. In 2004 and 2005 I took part in the international festival of fashion, the *Kiev Podium*, as a designer of clothes and accessories made of leather. I won third place in the category "fantasy" for one dress I created and called *Crystal Silhouette*.

AOM: When did you first want to be an artist?
V.G.: I remember as a child, thirteen years old, I was amazed when I saw a photo of the painting by Raphael, the *Sistine Madonna*. I even attempted to paint it myself. And then in 2012 I went to Germany and visited the world famous Dresden Gallery of Old Masters. I saw the *Sistine Madonna* for the first time—the original—and I was struck so much by this painting, its inner radiance, that I could not hold back the tears. Here it is—the magic power of art in action!

Goryaev, *Adam,* oil on canvas, 120 x 55 cm. 2014

Goryaev, example of body-art

AOM: What challenges you as an artist?
V.G.: I like to work with nude male models. It has always been the most challenging for me to capture hands, as they are very expressive, and eyes, a mirror of the soul. And I love painting on the naked body–body-art. It's exciting when you see how the body changes its line and character under the brush.

AOM: If you could own one work of art, and price was no issue, what would it be?
V.G.: If I could buy any painting in the world at my desire, I would like a later self-portrait of Rembrandt–he is greatest of all artists in the world of art in my opinion.

Goryaev, *Sitter*, pencil on paper, 50 x 30 in. 1989

Goryaev, *Morning*, oil on canvas, 80 x 50 in. 1995

AOM: Do you collect art?
V.G.: I'm very fond of pottery and I collect it. I have a small collection of cups that I bought myself. Even my friends bring me interesting cups as a gift from their travels.

AOM: What advice would you give to artists?
V.G.: I advise young beginner artists of only one thing, to create without looking back, to search for and develop individuality in itself, that is a quality that should have a "real artist."

To see more of the artist's work, please visit his website at: goryaev.com.ua

Goryaev, *Seated Sitter*, pencil, 40 x 30 in. 1989

Cody Furguson

Art of Man: Tell us about yourself Cody.
Cody Furguson: I'm from Oklahoma and I paint men. I studied graphic art in high school. I was a web-designer in the early 2000s, then switched to fine art.

AOM: Why is the male figure a significant part of your portfolio?
C.F.: It's what I'm attracted to. I'm also insulted, as a gay man, that the male figure is less accepted in the art world than the female figure. I see it as an issue of discrimination.

AOM: What is it about your technique or approach that sets your work apart from other artists working with the male figure?
C.F.: I think of my work as two dimensional sculpture. Form is absolutely critical to me. I want each painting to "feel" right. I'm also a bit of a scientist. I'm always experimenting with original, novel techniques. I will try anything to get the desired results. I've invented many interesting processes, although I don't use them all now.

Lately I've been working with masonite panels. I usually use the absorbent side because I like the way it dries. It gives the painting a "pastel-like" finish. It's similar to the way Francis Bacon painted on the backside of his canvases. The paint absorbs into it, which is completely different than the smooth side.

Left: Furguson, Smokescreen, oil, 36 x 24 in.
Next Pages: Furguson, Safe Haven, oil, 24 x 36 in.
 (image slightly cropped)

It's very close to painting oil-on-cardboard, which looks wonderful and may even last but is way too flimsy. Oil on paper works have survived since the nineteenth century, so I'm not worried about longevity there. Oil on masonite has been around since the 1940's at least with no known deterioration. That said, I also like to work on hand-gessoed canvas and linen.

AOM: Have you encountered any issues about having the male figure in your work?
C.F.: Oh, yes. I find that delivery people get nosy and open my work. Sometimes they destroy it or even make annoying comments. Of course, I live in a small red-neck town. I've had to switch carriers a few times, but I finally started making my packages nearly indestructible with foam insulation panels and wads of duct tape.

AOM: Do you see a change in the acceptance of the male figure as subject?
C.F.: It's not what it should be. Why are naked women fine and naked men not? Marriage equality should help with that over time, but the only real solution is smarter people.

AOM: Where do you hope to see your work going in ten or twenty years?
C.F.: In ten years I want male-themed nudes accepted in the best galleries. All galleries. In twenty years I want straight men hanging male nudes on their walls without shame.

Above: Furguson, *Decadence*, oil, 24 x 36 in.

Left: Furguson, *Regency*, oil, 36 x 24 in.

AOM: Have you always worked in this style?
C.F.: Pretty much. I started out as a cartoonist. Then my aunt talked me into painting blues-singers on ties. They were very similar to the style I use now, but much smaller. I hate painting small now.

AOM: How long does it take to complete a work?
C.F.: The easier a painting is the better it is. Most of my paintings take—honestly—a day's worth of solid labor—three at the most. If a painting takes a week, it's probably really iffy. There are exceptions.

AOM: Who would be your inspirations as an artist?
C.F.: John Singer Sargent and Jeremy Lipking. They're very similar, one past and one present. I have so many inspirations and influences it's hard to name them all.

AOM: Do you have a humorous experience you can share related to your work, studio, model, or client?
C.F.: A former roommate—very cute and supposedly straight—got drunk, he kicked in my bedroom door when I was in the shower, passed out on my bed beneath the painting *Smoke Screen*. He woke up a few minutes later and left before I got out. My door jam is still broken in three pieces.

The next day he claimed the painting was of him—which it was not. He said I should give the painting to him. Later, he broke into my room again, stole the painting and kept it at his new house with his girlfriend for over a day. I spent the day begging him in phone messages to bring it back because it had sold for a lot of money and I had to ship it out.

Furguson, *Radiance*, oil, 24 x 24 in.

AOM: Where do you find your models?
C.F.: Grindr. Models, husbands, sex. You can get it all on Grindr. But you have to be really careful. Grindr is a soul-sucking black hole of time wasting. Especially in Oklahoma. The hours I've spent, anguished, waiting for someone to respond to the question, "Can I paint you sometime?"

AOM: Tell us about your very first exhibition.
C.F.: I've never had one. I always sell everything online to pay the bills. That's why I've always been broke.

AOM: Do you remember your first art sale?
C.F.: Yes. It was a very modern air-brushed piece. Something like a giant purple metallic marble. I sold it then tried to improve it and wound up ruining it. I still got paid though, because I was a kid and they felt sorry for me.

AOM: When did you want to become an artist?
C.F.: When I got the Maurice Sendak book *Where the Wild Things Are*. It all stems from that. What a perfect thing. So rare when you're a kid for something to live up to your expectations, and even surpass them. When I found out he was gay, years later, I was surprised and thrilled.

AOM: When sales are down, what have you done to support yourself?
C.F.: I rent my house out. I rent out 4 rooms and live in the converted garage/studio which I love. Income property is where it's at.

AOM: Have you ever been brought to tears in front of a work of art?
C.F.: Absolutely not. If a work of art is really amazing I just get jealous. I think, "I'm going to be able to do that someday."

Prodigies are the worst.

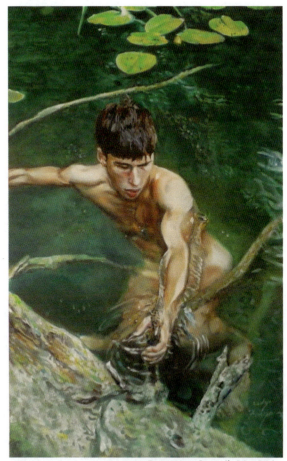
Furguson, *Coy*, oil, 36 x 24 in.

Furguson, *White Stripes*, oil, 24 x 24 in.

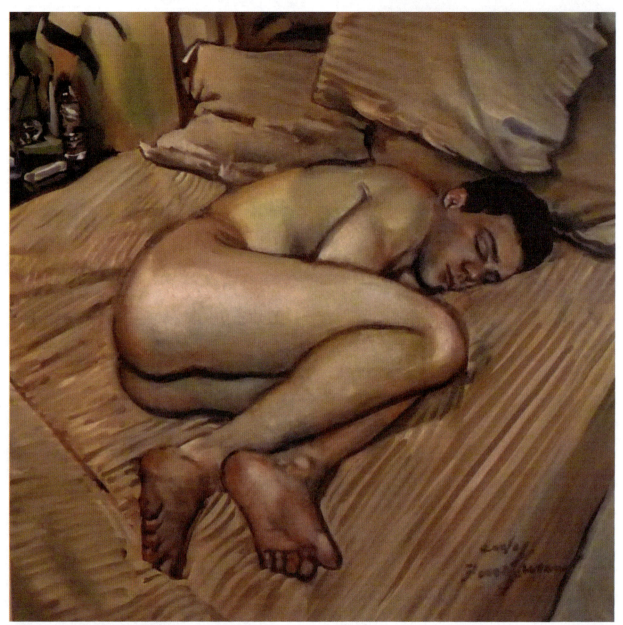

Furguson, *Light Sleeper*, oil, 24 x 24 in.

AOM: Do you collect art?
C.F.: Only virtual art. I did Pinterest until I thought I'd collected about everything I like. It also helped me solidify exactly what I admire in paintings. "The five C's.": Content, Composition, Contrast, Color Balance, and Clarity.

AOM: What advice would you give younger artists?
C.F.: If you have talent and persistence you can make a living as a fine artist, especially today with all the online selling venues. Keep your work and sell prints. I'm still working on that one.

Furguson, *Possibilities*, oil, 36 x 24 in.

AOM: If you could wave a magic wand and anyone in the world would appear to be your next model, who would that dream model be?

C.F.: Somehow the porn star Brent Everett friended me on Facebook. To my knowledge I never requested him as a friend and didn't even realize until recently that he was on my friend list. Maybe he friends all gay people, I don't know. Anyway, I think he's beautiful. One night, I got really drunk and wrote that I wanted to take care of him and protect him from the world! Ha. One of the great privileges of being an artist is the right to go insane now and then.

AOM: Without burning any bridges can you share a best or worst experience in a gallery or with a client?

C.F.: Many years ago I took a really beautiful rustic pen-and-ink drawing of mine—of a train—to a gallery. It was perfectly framed and matted and looked really nice and I'd won a lot of awards for it in high school. The Gallery Owner was very snobby about it and wouldn't consider taking it because I wasn't a "known artist." That's probably why the Internet was so attractive to me. No middle-men.

AOM: What subject is the most challenging for you as an artist to capture.

C.F.: Faces and hands. Everything else is gravy. I learned from Jeremy Lipking "Take as much time on faces as you have to." They usually take three or four times longer than anything else. I'm pretty good with hands now. To me that was Picasso's one saving grace. He could really draw fingers and toes—at least in the early days when he still tried.

AOM: If you could own just one work of art, which one would it be? Pretend money is not an issue.

C.F.: My abstract painting *"Storm the Arctic."* I couldn't do without it. I sold the first version which was in 2 panels 24 X 36 inches each—and then had to repaint it. The second version is better and one single 48 X 36 inches a piece. All the paintings in my living room are abstracts by me. I have a real talent for abstracts, but no time.

AOM: Do you have a secret talent?

C.F.: I'm a musician, singer, and writer. I used to do a "song a day" podcast, but the song productions kept getting more and more complicated and taking longer. When I ran out of money one time they locked me out and I said, "fuck it. This is too much work for no money." I'm currently working on an epic Sci-fi TV series with my favorite cute-straight roommate, Zack. We're also going to start a band.

Someday I will make movies. I'd like to make a movie about Tommy Kirk, the gay Disney actor who starred in Old Yeller and The Shaggy Dog. He made Disney a lot of money and then was treated really poorly back when the studio was ultra-conservative.

Apparently he had a lot of the boys on the lot in his trailer as a kid and wasn't too discreet about it. I'm just drawn to his story, his guts in the face of "how things are and must be." It's just more "Wild Things."

Please visit the artist's website for his newest work and additional information at:
www.codyfurguson.com

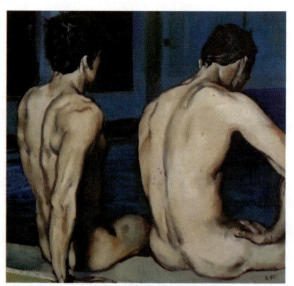

Above: Furguson, *Mates*, oil, 24 x 24 in.
Right: Furguson, *Blind Faith*, oil, 36 x 24 in.

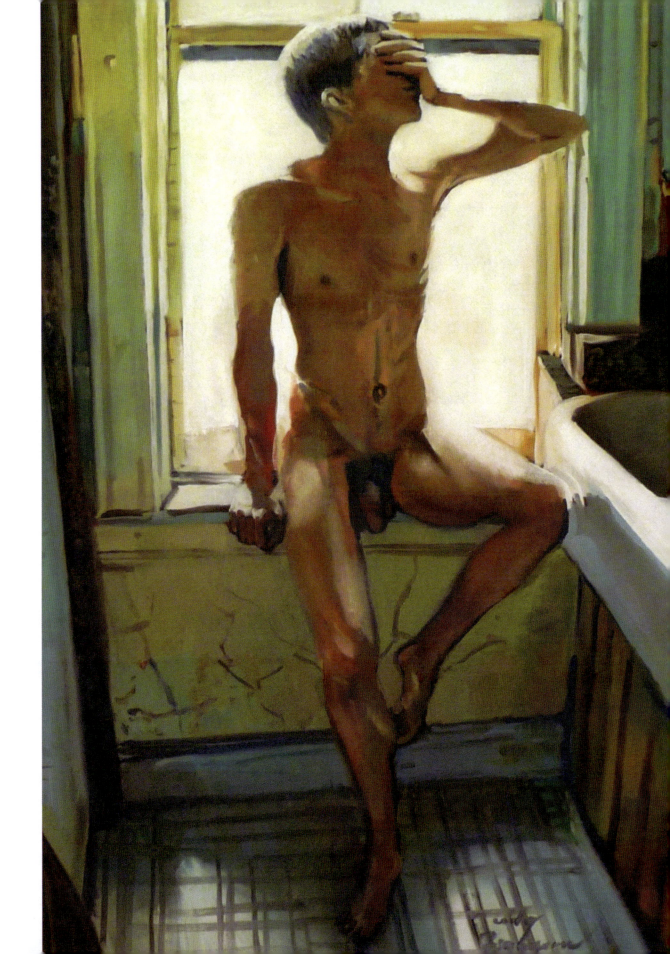

LIZARDI/HARP
GALLERY

626.791.8123 lizardiharp@earthlink.net

Wes Hempel, Gerard Huber, José Parra, Wade Reynolds

Huber, *Classical Figures XV Sapere aude*, acrylic on masonite panel, 39 X 60 in. 2006

Huber, *Reflections I*, acrylic on masonite panel, 27 X 46 in. 2013

Paul Rybarczyk
Contemporary figure paintings and portraits

Paul Rybarczyk is a Licensed Massage Therapist who works with the human body in more than one way. Besides manipulating the body with his hands, he also is an artist who visually manipulates the body in color and on paper and canvas, creating artwork featuring the male figure.

Commissions accepted.

www.artworkbypaul.com
Paul Rybarczyk • Buffalo, NY

John Singer Sargent
1856-1925

JOHN SINGER SARGENT
Edwardian luxury and altering sensibilities
By Grady Harp

"Art is the most intense mode of individualism that the world has known." ~Oscar Wilde

John Singer Sargent is considered an American artist but like so many aspects of his life even his designated country of origin has variations. He was born in 1856 in Florence, Italy to American parents, but his childhood was spent travelling throughout Europe. His father had been an ophthalmologist in Philadelphia, but when John's older sister died at age two his mother collapsed psychologically and the couple decided to move abroad. They remained nomadic expatriates for the rest of their lives. Although based in Paris, Sargent's parents moved regularly with the seasons to the sea and the mountain resorts in France, Germany, Italy, and Switzerland. Sargent's artistic proclivity began at a young age, and his parents, realizing his talent, enrolled him in art classes in Florence at the Accademia delle Belle Arti, in his late teens. During the winter of 1873-74, Sargent polished his skills and his father was convinced that it was well worth encouraging his son's artistic pursuits.

Left: Sargent, *Dr Jean Pozzi at Home*, 1881

Father and son traveled together to Paris in the spring of 1874 where on the first attempt, Sargent passed the rigorous exam required to gain admission to the École des Beaux-Arts and took drawing classes, which included anatomy and perspective, gaining a silver prize.

Sargent, *Standing Male Figure*, charcoal on paper

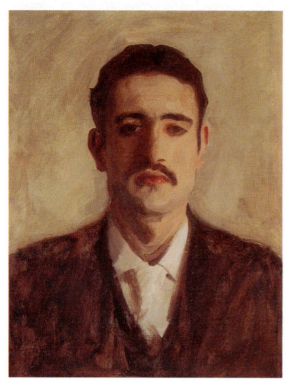

Sargent, *Study Portrait of Nicola d'Inverno,* 1888

Sargent, *Sketch for Apollo and the Muses*, graphite and charcoal on paper, 1917

Sargent travelled extensively as his paintings document. He enjoyed international acclaim as a portrait painter but also created both controversy and some critical reservation. A trip to Madrid in 1879 inspired the masterpiece of his youth, *El Jaleo* (1882) depicting the passion and sensuality of flamenco dance. Earthy and exotic, it created a scandal when exhibited, alerting the artistic establishment of his nature. And with this tendency to create paintings that shocked, he created the famous full-length portrait of New Orleans beauty Virginie Gautreau in a strapless black gown with a plunging neckline which was eviscerated by the critics as scandalous—'a depiction of a sexually aware and desiring woman and as a comment on Parisian social pretensions.' Sargent eventually changed the title to *Portrait of Madame X* to protect the sitter.

Further controversy followed the unveiling of his portrait of womanizing gynecologist Dr. Samuel Jean Pozzi at Home (1881) in his dressing gown. To escape the scandal created by the Portrait of Madame X, Sargent moved to London in 1886, where he eventually established a brilliant career as a society and celebrity portraitist—the most popular portrait painter of his day with many famous people considering it de rigueur to commission him for portraits.

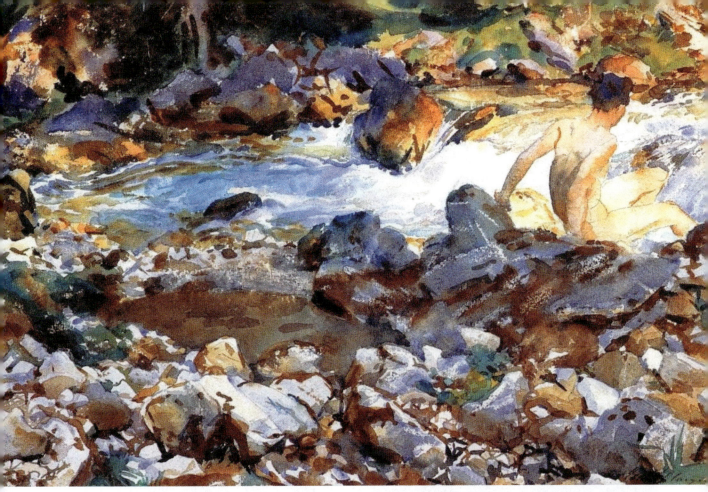

Sargent, *Mountain Stream,* watercolor on paper, 1904

Sargent, *On His Holiday-Norway*, oil on canvas, 1901

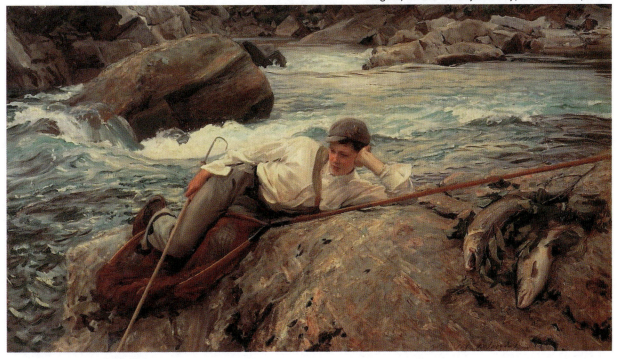

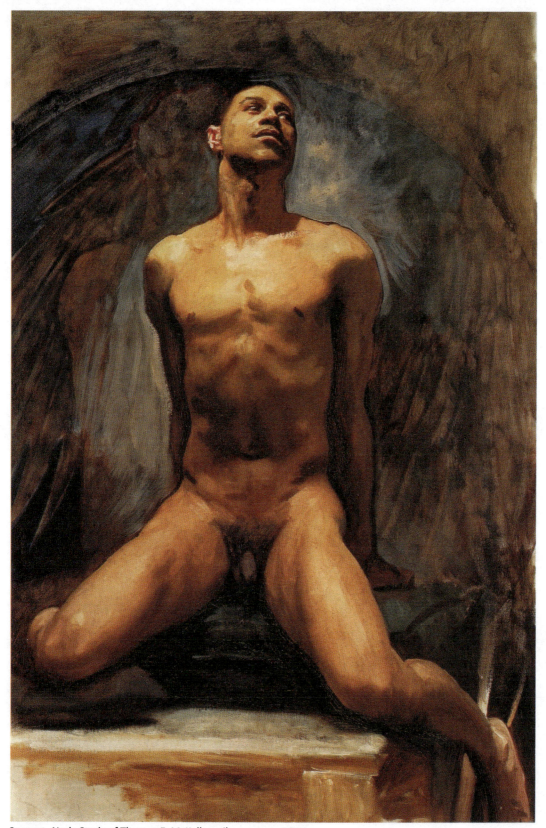

Sargent, *Nude Study of Thomas E. McKeller*, oil on canvas, 1917

Sargent, *Nude in Trees*, watercolor on paper, 1917

The wealthy, famous, and noble on both sides of the Atlantic flocked to the London studio of this expatriate American, sealing his reputation as one of the most famous and recognizable of American artists. Included among his portraits are those of Robert Louis Stevenson, Theodore Roosevelt, and Woodrow Wilson. These still famous portraits sold for high prices and provided a comfortable life and career, yet the repetitive assembly line nature of the work increasingly dissatisfied him. From 1900 to 1907 he painted about 15 to 25 portraits annually.

From his earliest work, in both paintings and drawings, his work demonstrated rather extraordinary technical facility, particularly in his ability to draw with a brush, which in later years inspired admiration as well as criticism for a supposed superficiality. His commissioned works were consistent with the grand manner of portraiture: his casual watercolor and drawing studies and landscape paintings

Sargent, *Gassed*, oil on canvas, 1918

acknowledged at least a familiarity with Impressionism: perhaps one of his most celebrated paintings is *Carnation, Lily, Lily, Rose* where two children play in the gloaming with lighted lanterns. Stepping away from his Impressionistic canvases, one of the idiosyncrasies of his other work is the tension between respectability and sensuality in his art, especially his ability to suggest the transgressive without actually violating social proprieties—and at times mirror of the similar tension in Sargent's personal life. Because of his ability to capture the essence of male power and female beauty without superficiality, Sargent is considered by some to be "vanity's butler" for making everyone appear dashing and beautiful. But his work is very frequently unsparingly candid, able to depict his sitters' insecurity and awkwardness as well as their beauty and power. The delicate brushwork, nuanced color, and ingenious use of setting make his portraits uniquely vibrant and alive.

Sargant, *The Bathers*, graphite watercolor and gouache on paper, 1917

Among Sargent's many friends were such luminaries as Henry James, Robert Louis Stevenson, Oscar Wilde, fellow painter Henry Scott Tuke, symbolist poet Robert de Montesquieu, and poet/literary critic John Addington Symonds, most of whom were homosexual (then usually called Uranian) and who celebrated the adolescent male. Yet to the general public and even to his friends he was known as distant and reserved. He had no great romantic attachments, only flirtations with women and deep friendships with men. Although it was rumored that his relationship with his long-time model and assistant Nicola d'Inverno went beyond camaraderie, no evidence of a physical liaison of any kind has been documented. When Sargent died in 1925, his family destroyed his personal papers, so the evidence for Sargent's homosexuality resides largely in his work, especially his genre paintings and male nudes–images that are quietly erotic with an unabashed attention to genitalia. Even in his mural *Triumph of Religion* (1890–1919) his figures of choice are young male bodies that offer the unfinished Boston Library mural a marked erotic flavor.

Sargent was very fond of his model Thomas E. McKeller, an African American blue collared Bostonian male of stunning physique whom Sargent painted as a full frontal nude in a large scale oil for his private viewing and never displayed to the public in his lifetime. It was known that Sargent was in the habit of looking

Sargent, *A Summer Idyll*, oil on cardboard, 1877

at men's bodies in public. While his true sexuality has been the subject of continuing controversy, critic Trevor Fairbrother has stated, "I would argue—though people may contest what constitutes evidence—that he was probably gay and very repressed. He led a double life, a public facade vs. the real person. The real person is hidden, as those who really knew were sworn to secrecy, sort of the way Hollywood still is today." Both McKellar and d'Inverno served as models for his copious number of male nudes for which he is only now becoming known. The painter Jacques-Émile Blanche, one of his early models, said after his death that Sargent's sex life "was notorious in Paris, and in Venice, positively scandalous. He was a frenzied bugger."

Setting aside the discussion of his sexual inclinations, John Singer Sargent remains one of the American iconic painters. His Edwardian portraits of the rich and famous can now be placed in full context with his numerous watercolors of Venice, his landscapes and seascapes, tributes to the war effort (as in *Gassed*, 1918) and his extraordinary images of the male nude. His impact is still being discovered as paintings are found in old private collections. His spirit—very much alive!

Sargent, *FigureStudy,* watercolor and graphite, 1904

Sargent, *Robert Gould Shaw III in Uniform,* 1923

Sargent, *Olimpio Fusco*, charcoal, 1905

Sargent, *Man with Red Drapery*, watercolor, 1904

"Only in men's imagination does every truth find an effective and undeniable existence. Imagination, not invention, is the supreme master of art as life." ~Joseph Conrad 1912

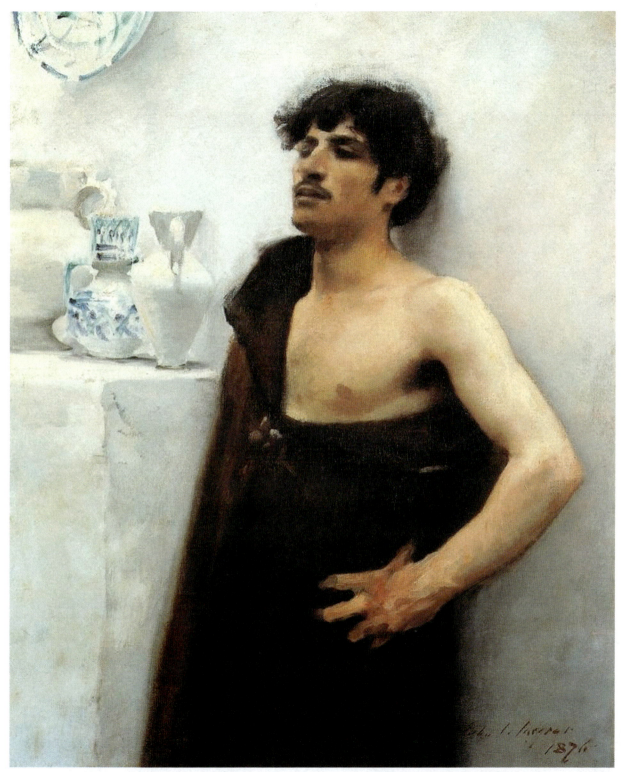

Sargent, *Young Man in Reverie*, oil on canvas, 1876

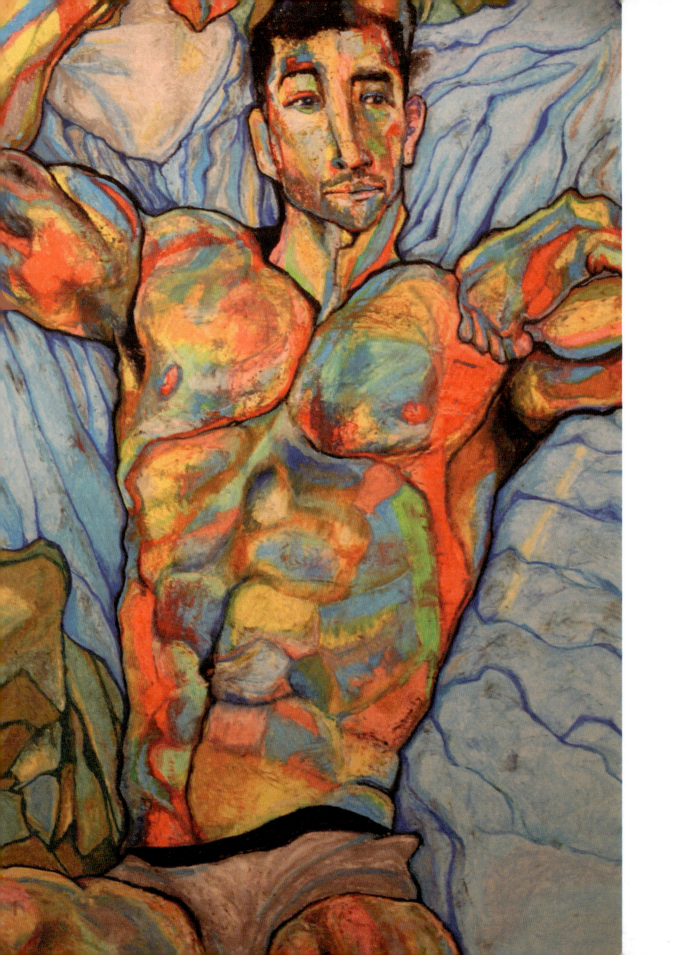

LIN JUN LIANG

Lian Jun Lin is from Taipei, Taiwan. As an artist he is known as Lin Jun Llang since last names are traditionally printed first. Jun (俊) translates to handsome, and Liang (良) to good. Appropriate for his work of *good handsome* men.

Art of Man: Please tell us a bit about yourself.
Lin Jun Llang: I'm a free-lance artist, most of my focus is selling my art. I make a living doing it. When I was in the university my major was 3D graphics and stop motion animation. In graduate school I studied video art and new art media. Presently, conceptual art is the main subject of my art work.

Drawing is my other necessary skill in order to keep my mind quiet and balanced. It's a very Asian tradition–to always pursue the Zen condition. In the future, I hope to become an art educator. So a PHD will be my next step to better my knowledge of art and to improve my strengths and capabilities.

AOM: Many figurative artists focus almost exclusively on the female form, why do you include more male figures n your portfolio?
LJL: I'm a gay man, I don't have any gift to draw female figures well. But I started to draw the male figure about ten years ago. I was taught to draw female figures when I was very young. One day I discovered the beauty of male bodies. That's when I changed my focus and medium.

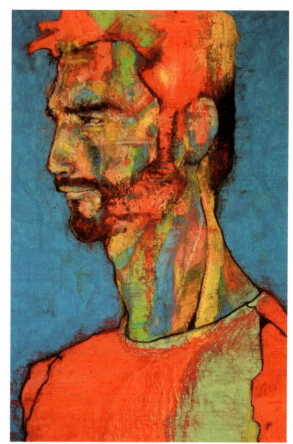

Above: Lin, *Untitled,* grease crayon, 2012

Left: Lin, *Untitled,* grease crayon, 2013

Above: Lin, *Untitled,* grease crayon, 2013

Right: Lin, *Untitled,* grease crayon, 2014

AOM: What is unique about your approach?
LJL: I seldom feel that I'm unique, most of time, I feel like I'm extremely insignificant.

AOM: Have you encountered any issues about having the male figure in your work?
LJL: Sometimes the male models become overly self-conscious, and it ruins the work. We just have to stop and change the schedule.

It happens a lot.

AOM: Where do you find your models?
LJL: Sometimes I find a great photograph or I use pictures I take of people on the street.

AOM: Culturally, it must be difficult to focus on the male form in a homophobic society. Maybe things will get better. Do you see a change in the acceptance of the male figure as subject?
LJL: The male figure is still considered a gay subject. It is not widely accepted but considered special. There are not many people doing it.

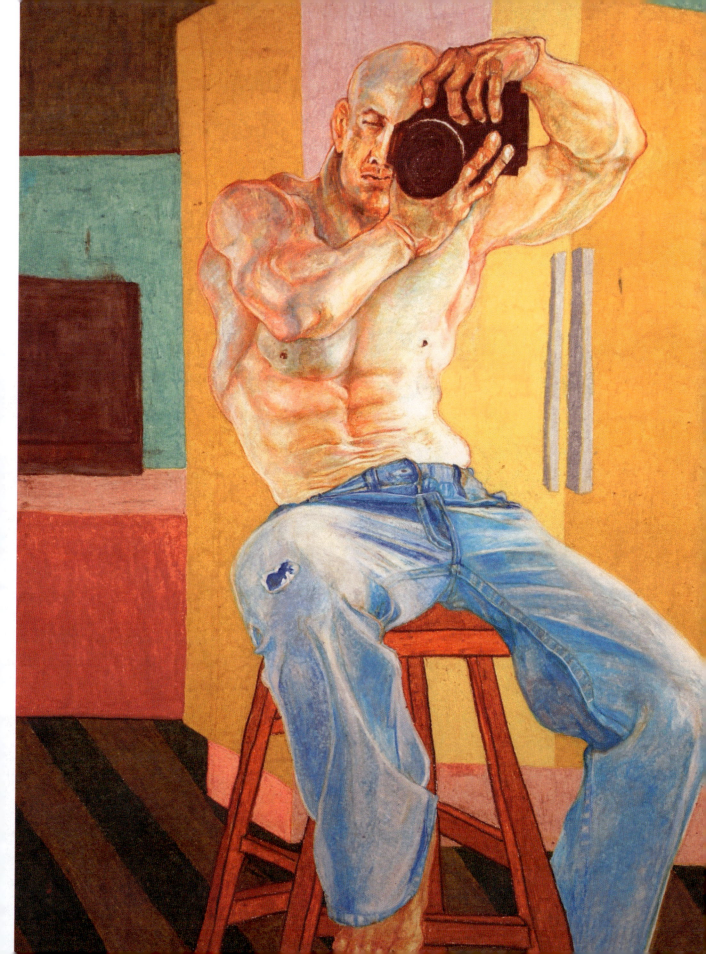

Lin, *Untitled,* grease crayon, 2013

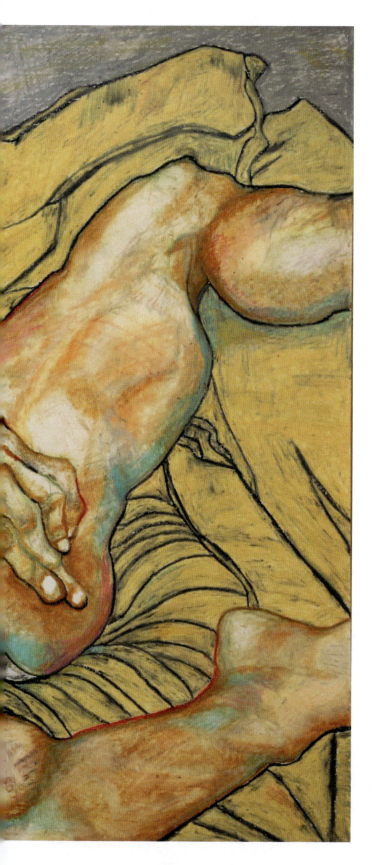

AOM: Do you have a humorous experience you can share related to your work?
LJL: For a long time I couldn't draw a penis to be perfect, I think the penis is totally out of body–figuratively speaking–very isolated with it's own personality. Usually it doesn't have the same personality as the person who owns it, but we're so preoccupied with it as if it had a soul. I focus on the eyes connecting with the viewer, they are always stronger than body. We connect with each other at the soul level, not through the muscles, or the penis.

AOM: We discovered your work through Tumblr. How do you feel when your work pops up on social websites?
LJL: Grateful. It is great that art can reach people like this, through pure luck and happenstance. It can also add an unexpected layer of pressure. To meet expectations about the male figure, the body, and my work.

AOM: How has your style developed?
LJL: I did my best to forget the drawing skills I learned when I was in school, to let go and discover a new way to use paint. I tried to invest more time and energy in the emotional content, but not through any specific style or mode. I seek perfection in my own eyes. When one of my friends introduced me to the work of Egon Schiele, it changed my life's work. I finally found a way to understand the *performance of art*, a method to connect to my unconscious mind. It is my approach now.

AOM: Tell me something people might not know about you or your work?
LJL: The most interesting thing is I don't plan or sketch. I don't over-work my art. I go straight away non-stop. I will work straight

through, sometimes ten hours. I spend a lot of time contemplating a piece before I begin, or thinking about future projects.

AOM: Who would be your artistic inspirations?
LJL: Strangely enough, the pianist Glenn Gould as well as Egon Schiele of course.

AOM: Tell us about your very first exhibition
LJL: My first exhibition was not drawing exhibit. It was a conceptual art exhibit. At that time lots of professional people came and judged my work seriously. After five years I finally had a drawing exhibit for the first time. Most of the visitors were around 25-35 years old. They did not judge my work but were fascinated by it.

AOM: When did you first want to be a artist?
LJL: When I was taking master courses my professor thought I was an artist with personal style and with my own way approaching subjects. I decided to be an artist, an outstanding artist.

AOM: Can you share a best or worst experience in a gallery or with a client?
LJL: The best experience was an international buyer who kept looking at an image from the internet through he was from very far away. Finally he found my agent and got this art piece. This experience made me feel very good that they went through so much trouble to acquire my work. But I was also surprised to learn he is not a *professional collector*.

As for a bad experience, there was a collector that said he was going to buy lot of my work, but in the end he didn't. It was mainly because he kept trying to negotiate a lower price. He also returned five pieces and told everyone my work is too expensive. I learned that passion can't be calculated by money.

AOM: Do you have a secret talent?
LJL: Playing piano.

Left: Lin, *Untitled,* grease crayon, 2013
Right: Lin, *Untitled,* grease crayon, 2013

AOM: Have you ever been brought to tears in front of a work of art?
LJL: The first time I saw a real Picasso's painting. A huge one, but I already forgot its name. It was very simple with only black lines and grey color bars, but he made me to feel his subject so deeply. I feel as though I totally understand what he saw with his eyes without any doubts.

AOM: What subject is the most challenging for you as an artist to capture?
LJL: Pictures with lots of people in the frame are the most challenging for me. I don't like to squeeze too many people and emotion into a single image. I love to focus on only one person's soul.

AOM: Who would your dream model be?
LJL: Daniel Wroughton Craig, the 007 actor.

For more information about the artists please visit www.cargocollective.com/linjunliang

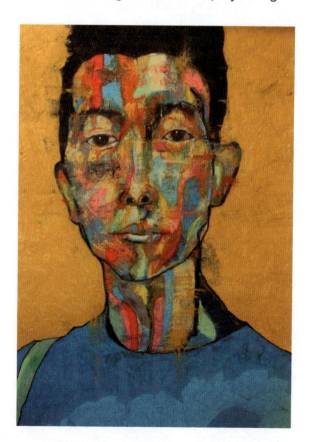

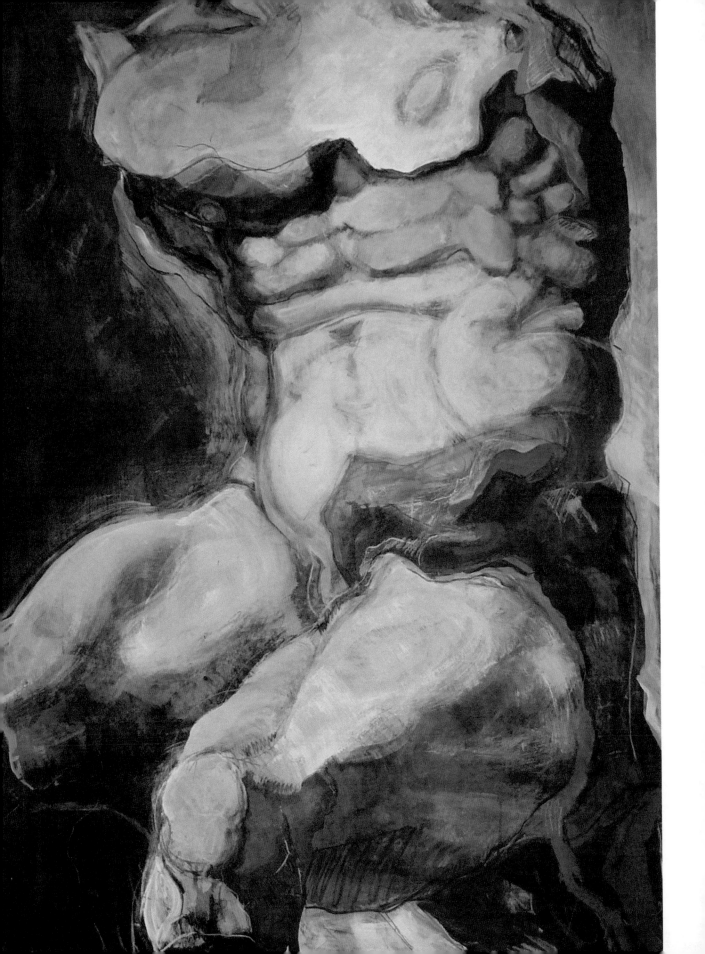

Rebecca Ivatts

Art of Man: Tell us about yourself and your work.
Rebecca Ivatts: I have exhibited my work in London, Madrid, Northern Spain, Athens, and Ireland.

The human figure—as a subject of great dynamism and emotional power—has always formed the basis for my work. In my work expression takes precedence over realism, and to maximize the presence and immediacy of my figures, I generally depict them at life-size scale or bigger. In fact, unlike most artists, I often find myself working from large to small instead of vice versa. Instead of realist flesh tones, I often opt for strong palettes incorporating black and white monochrome and red.

After living in Madrid for four years and spending so much time in the Prado and Reina Sofia, major influences include Goya, El Greco, Ignacio Zuloaga, Picasso, and Antonio Saura.

Most of my work seeks some ambiguity and expressive, organic quality in the juxtaposition of figures, be they intertwined bodies, wrestling males or kissing heads. I love to flip the figure round and free it from gravity to create interesting dimensions. Hence, two kissing heads become more like an exciting landscape or abyss, and a kneeling male suspended in space resembles a brain.

In addition to anatomy, my work increasingly draws on science and technology including cosmology, astrophysics, quantum, Big Bang, and dark matter theories as well as neuroscience and fluid dynamics. In a sense, I want to feel my way towards a new science-informed spirituality while staying within the great tradition of European figure painting.

AOM: Why is the male figure a significant part of your portfolio?
R.I.: The male figure features strongly in my work because I simply love it. I grew up looking at my (artist) godfather's amazing male life drawings of his own torso and arms and just adored that strength. I always felt the male figure had greater expressive possibilities than the female than has been represented in fine art so much more.

AOM: What is it about your technique or approach that sets your work apart from other artists working with the male figure?
R.I.: I guess that where my work is most successful it refers back to the great artists of the male form—Michelangelo, Rodin, etc—while taking on board contemporary methods, mediums, supports, etc. In some cases, contemporary concepts too—such as the male figures in my Dark Matter series.

Left: Ivatts, *Belvedere Diptych*, mixed media, 175 x 270 cm. 2008

Ivatts, *Butterfly*, acrylic, 121 x 152 cm. 2012

AOM: Have you encountered any issues about having the male figure in your work?
R.I.: Normally the response has been positive and the strength of my figures is often commented on. Funnily enough however, I had a show in Spain once and a newspaper critic resorted to some cod psychology in his article saying it was as though I projected my identity on to the male and perhaps had gender identity issues. I actually felt this was a gross oversimplification as we all embody a male and female part. My love of the male form is not a straight projection of my sexual desires either—as, traditionally, it often was in the case of many or even most male painters.

AOM: Do you see a change in the acceptance of the male figure as subject?
R.I.: Yes, as I have just said we perhaps have a more fluid and open conception of gender and the nude now. We also live in times when it's difficult to shock. Ironically, I feel that true tenderness, humanity, and love could come as more of a shock in an artwork now than sex, pornography, or violence.

AOM: Do you have a humorous experience you can share related to your work, studio, model, or client?
R.I.: One model I used in Spain a few years ago was so proud of my immortalization of him on canvas—I played down his receding hairline and short height—

Ivatts, *Dark Matter 1*, acrylic, 140 x 180 cm. 2010

that he still uses the image of him for Facebook and Twitter, etc. to this day!

Also, when I used to paint from live models at the Circulo de Bellas Artes in Madrid, I found it hilarious that the principal would come in with a textbook of life model poses and choose one for the next pose. They were dreadful, old-fashioned, predictable, concrete poses that you sensed they'd been using for hundreds of years!

AOM: What is in the future for your work?

R.I.: It's hard to say where my work will be in a decade or two as I'm not a one-trick pony and am forever trying new ideas. I applied my knowledge of anatomy to the arthritic hands of my godfather not long ago and after attending hand lectures in the dissection room of Guy's Hospital in London, I produced vast canvases of his hands. At the risk of sounding immodest, I haven't seen any such large and strong depictions of hands by other artists in recent years. Recently, I've been painting some grey matter portraits constructed from fMRI brain scans. It's funny though, I always come back to the figure and know that it's what I do best.

AOM: Have you always worked in this style?
R.I.: I guess that my draftsmanship underpins everything I do and always has. The difference is that I'm now into pushing paint around and really making the medium work. Despite this I think there is a continuum in my work.

AOM: Tell me something people might not know about you or your work?
R.I.: I have an innate propensity to do things life-size, if not bigger. Unlike the vast majority of artists, I instinctively work VERY large and if need be have to rein myself in to scale down and produce smaller works or drawings!

AOM: Where do you find your models?
R.I.: In Spain I had loads of models happy to pose in return for English conversation. I loved that, sometimes we even sat and did grammar after a session. One poor model had to virtually stand on her head for one painting I did of falling figures. If money and space were no matter, I'd love to rig scaffolding in a huge studio and have models hang off it and defy gravity.

AOM: Tell us about your very first exhibition.
R.I.: My first proper solo exhibition was in Madrid at Galeria Tribeca which, due to the economic recession, no longer exists. They painted the walls black and each of my works—large works of predominantly male bodies in movement—shone like a colored jewel against the somber backdrop.

AOM: Do you remember your first art sale?
R.I.: The first works sold were in London through not the most wholesome looking dealer. He was an unshaven East-end geezer and kept wedges of cash in his paint-covered apron. I never quite accounted for all my drawings and their whereabouts. In the end I gave up on trying to chase the last few works.

AOM: Who would be your inspirations as an artist?
R.I.: Michelangelo, Caravaggio, Rodin, Schiele, Freud, Bacon, and Jenny Saville.

AOM: When did you first want to be an artist?
R.I.: I guess it was a slow process, not some overnight realization. I remember my godfather warning me: "Prepare to live on the margins of society!" When the UK collector Charles Saatchi said he liked my work, I thought the goal of becoming of a (successful) artist might finally be in sight.

AOM: What subject is the most challenging for you as an artist to capture?
R.I.: I guess the human figure never ceases to challenge me so that's why I love it. It could challenge me for several lifetimes.

Left: Ivatts, *Guantanamo Diptych 1*, mixed media, 2008

Ivatts, *Guantanamo Diptych 2*, mixed media, 2008

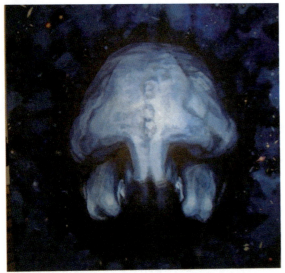
Ivatts, *Dark Matter IV*, acrylic, 150 x 150 cm. 2010

AOM: Without burning any bridges can you share a best or worst experience in a gallery?
R.I.: One Spanish gallery sold a work of mine but I had since moved back to London. I got a trusted friend to go and claim the cash but they had upped and left the premises and it was all shuttered up and abandoned.

AOM: When sales are down, what have you done to support yourself?
R.I.: I do some freelance arts, culture and travel journalism, some Spanish translation, and I also create portraits of children. For the latter, I've found they're really popular with American clients who like the drawings mounted on a vintage union jack flag.

AOM: If you could own just one work of art, which one would it be? Pretend money is not an issue.
R.I.: Tricky question. Maybe El Greco's *Resurrection* or Rembrandt's *Descent from the Cross*. Sculpture-wise, even just the right hand and wrist of Michelangelo's *David*. Without doubt, the most beautiful hand in the history of art.

AOM: What advice would you give to artists?
R.I.: Don't get too overwhelmed by all the other stuff out there and never underestimate the value of hard work. In the case of the nude, it hasn't been so popular in painting and is sometimes viewed as something elementary or old-fashioned. You have to ignore this sort of thing and plough on. *To thine own self be true.*

AOM: Where should readers go to see your work and/or contact you or your designated gallery?
R.I.: To see my work, www.rebeccaivatts.com or email me at beccaivatts@hotmail.com.

Artist in her studio with painting

Right: Ivatts, *Belvedere Diptych*, mixed media, 175 x 270 cm. 2008

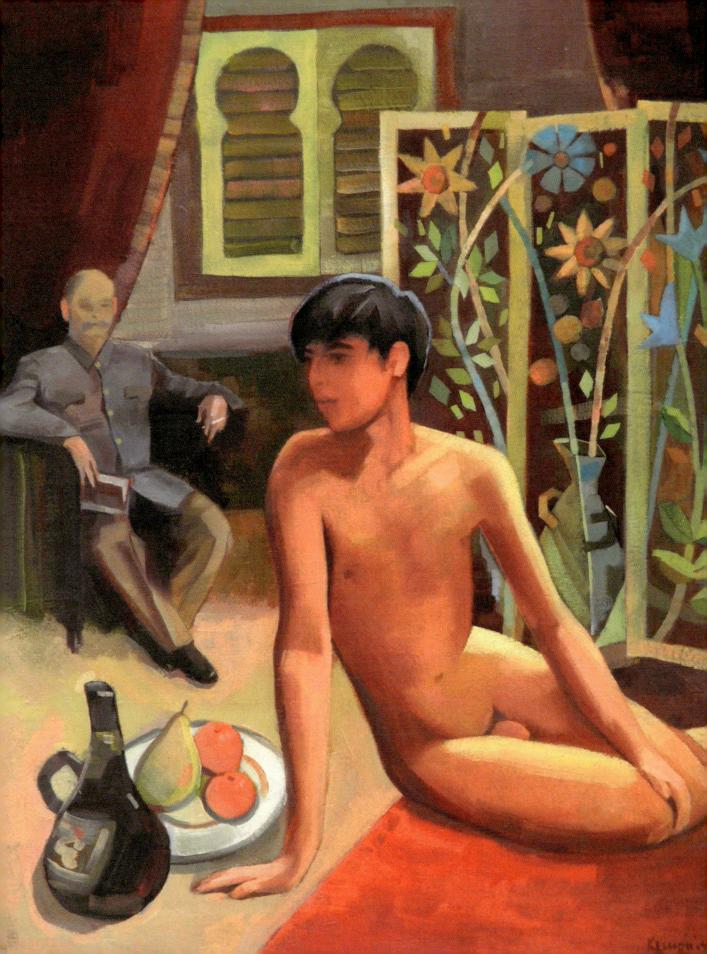

Maciej Kempinski

Art of Man: Tell us a bit about yourself.
Maciej Kempinski: I am a member of Polish Artists Painters and Graphic Designers Association and take part in exhibitions organized by the Association.

I paint landscapes, portraits, copies, and willingly, nudes. In some works I try to express the meaning through symbols. Sometimes I create the kind of tension juxtaposing opposites but at the same time I pay attention to color harmony and the whole form with a specific atmosphere.

AOM: Why do you focus on the male figure?
M.K.: I like young men and painting them is an expression of my fascination. In addition, it gives me the opportunity to express other feelings that I was not aware of when I was painting the pictures. I only realized these feelings existed when I began to talk to people about my work.

AOM: What are these feelings?
M.K.: Loneliness, longing, frustration...

AOM: What is it about your technique or approach that sets your work apart from other artists working with the male figure?
M.K.: That's a tough question...I think my work has some repetitive, recognizable features, although I am aware that I paint in different styles. Sometimes I like to paint spontaneously without a model, with only an idea in my head, with clean, sharp color. This gives me the pleasure of a quiet, systematic, operation. By contrast, with larger formats where the image is created based on a sketch, the fun comes from finding colors, creating inferences, and so on. In my paintings you can also find references to the techniques of other, often extremely different painters, work I admire and appreciate.

AOM: Have you encountered any issues about having the male figure in your work?
M.K.: No, but perhaps because I do not flaunt my works. Only a handful of friends and people interested in the male form know about what I paint. In Poland, after all, this kind of creativity meets with stigma. For example, my father says he would gladly share my website address with friends and extended family but because of my focus on the male figure he does not do it...

When it comes to the times and culture of the West, I think that there are no major problems. In Poland, however, as I have mentioned, despite greater acceptance for this kind of expression, it remains something marginal, a creative niche. You would not find a study of the male form hanging on the wall of your average gallery between a landscape and a still life.

Left: Kempinski, *Old Style Nude*, oil, 50 x 40 cm. 2008

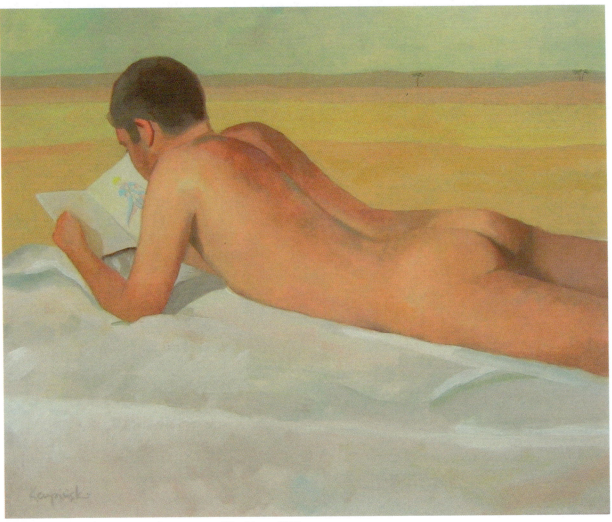

Kempinski, *The Little Prince*, acrylic on canvas, 50 x 61 cm. 2010

AOM: Do you have a humorous experience you can share related to your work, studio, model or client?
M.K.: Perhaps for some the funniest thing is that I do not actually have a studio—I just paint in the room I live in. A situation that upset me at first but which I could finally see the funny side of was when one of my paintings was stolen from a gallery. As a result the gallery gave me some compensation and it was also pleasing to think that someone liked the image so much that they decided to steal it!

AOM: Where do you hope to see your work going in 10 or 20 years?
M.K.: I don't want to run out of ideas by thinking too much about painting. My inspiration is in the "here and now." I'm just trying to grow, change, observe, and not stand still.

AOM: Tell me something people might not know about you or your work?
M.K.: It's a very personal question...I don't like to give too much of myself away, instead I prefer that people be interested in my paintings. One thing that cannot be seen in my work, something that has

Kempinski, *Let's Go*, oil on canvas, 50 x 70 cm. 2010

really bothered me through my life and even hinders my painting is obsessive neurosis. For some people, passion can be a refuge from their problems, they can find solace there. In my case, painting is a struggle with myself, because neurosis is trying to give me answers to the things that are most important to me, but painting such things would be discordant. Despite this, I still have to find a way somehow. It is very difficult...

AOM: Who would be your inspirations as an artist?
M.K.: I love many artists: Caravaggio, Lautrec, van Gogh, Balthus, Monet, and de Lempicka to name but a few. Impressionism, German Expressionism, Colorism, art nouveau, interwar Polish painting, and so on–these all inspire me. I also like the work of contemporary painters dealing with a very masculine subject, such as Cornelius McCarthy.

AOM: Without burning any bridges can you share a best or worst experience in a gallery or with a client?
M.K.: A great experience for me was meeting with Mr. Krzysztof, the well-known collector of Polish paintings. He was in my house and bought some of my work. I am very proud that my images are in a collection alongside works by some of the greatest Polish painters in history.

AOM: Where do you find your models?
M.K.: Frequently on dating sites. I ask them to pose, sometimes someone throws himself at me. A model has to inspire me; I need to be able to "see" something in my imagination in the form of an image. Sometimes I take pictures on the street and the 'model' does not even know about it. I can also be inspired by someone's picture in a magazine, a book, or in an advertisement.

Sometimes I draw looking at a live model. It's hard to arrange long sessions, unless you use an alla prima technique. Most often I paint from photos that were taken at previous modeling sessions.

AOM: Do you exhibit regularly?
M.K.: I have had the opportunity to have solo exhibitions but my work is also included in exhibitions organized by the Union of Artists, to which I belong.

AOM: Do you remember your first art sale?
M.K.: About twelve years ago. It was a portrait of an old Jew. It was probably not very successful in retrospect.

AOM: When did you first want to be an artist?
M.K.: From childhood I liked to draw and paint. When I was sixteen, I found a box of old oil paints in the trash in the yard. Finding this was the turning point for me. That was when my painting adventure seriously began.

AOM: Do you have a secret talent?
M.K.: I am quite musical and apparently even have a nice singing voice. I also used to write a lot of poems, some of which were printed. On the other hand, when it comes to dancing, I have two left feet!

AOM: What is the most difficult to capture?
M.K.: I think the biggest challenge for me as a painter is not one particular subject, but to transfer something elusive and multidimensional to my viewing audience.

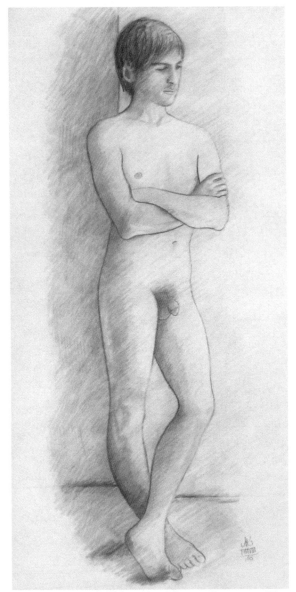

Above: Kempinski, *Without the Title*, pencil on paper, 74 x 50 cm. 2008 (cropped)

Right: Kempinski, *The Nude with a Bath*, acrylic on canvas, 100 x 81 cm. 2009

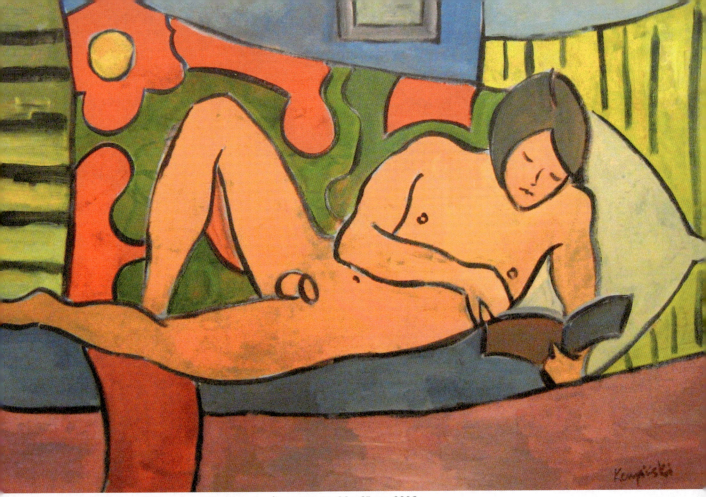

Kempinski, *Sexual Transportet Diseases*, acrylic on canvas, 96 x 65 cm. 2006

AOM: If you could own just one work of art, which one would it be? Pretend money is not an issue.
M.K.: If I had to choose, it would be a sculpture of a kneeling boy by Georges Minne which is very beautiful in its stylized, Art Nouveau form.

I don't collect art—I don't need to. The ability to be in contact with art is enough for me. I like to observe pictures, standing in the same spot where Renoir or Monet once stood, aware that I am looking at the same brush stoke they did all those years ago. That is a pleasant thrill that is enough for me.

AOM: What advice would you give to other artists?
M.K.: The most important things are a passion and knowledge. One without the other will always be incomplete, limited. Those who have a passion but no education, will not be able to fully express themselves as they will not have the tools. On the other hand someone who has a formal education, but no passion may create correct, even beautiful forms but these will soulless, empty, and lacking energy.

Picasso had something to say about the difference between an artist and an artisan: *"The artist sells what he paints; the artisan paints what sells."* I think it is important to get to know the works of old masters, learn from the experiences of other artists, but to seek your own individuality, your own way of painting, to be true to yourself, and not simply to follow fashion.

Right: Kempinski, *Boy and the Vasel*, oil, 55 x 38 cm. 2009

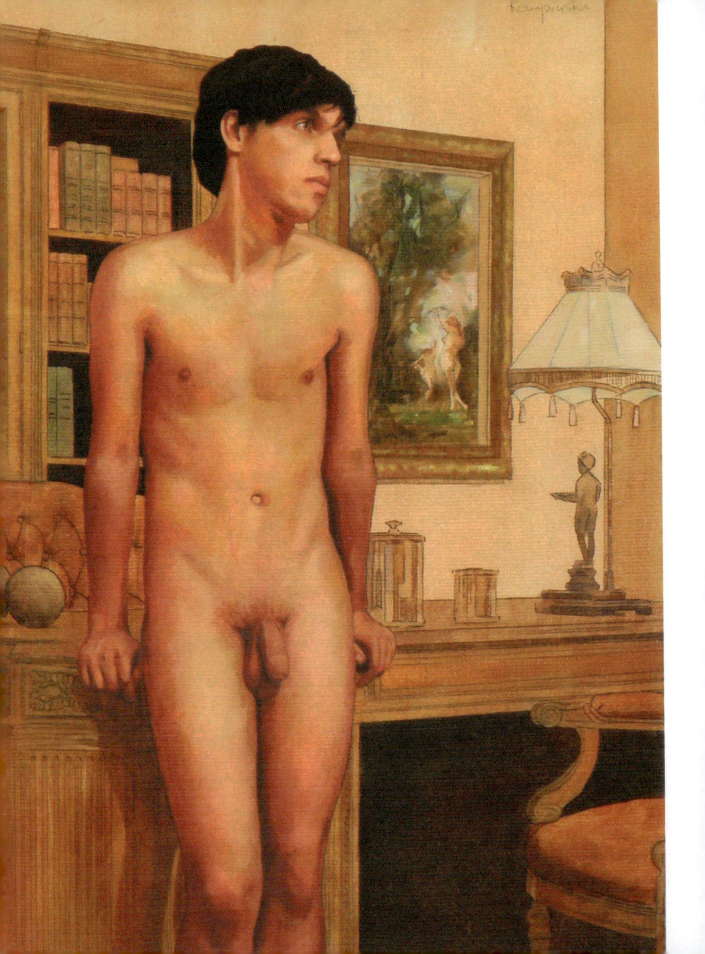

Kempinski, *Rather Late Afternoon*, acrylic, 50 x 40 cm. 2010

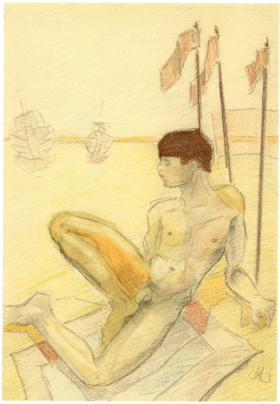

Kempinski, *Untitled*, pencil pastel on paper, 27 x 20 cm. 2008
Left Page: Kempinski, *Chef On Holiday*, oil, 46 x 33 cm. 2011

Kempinski, *White Shirt*, oil, 55 x 38 cm. 2013

AOM: If you could wave a magic wand and anyone in the world could be your next male model, who would that be?

M.K.: My first thought was Justin Bieber, but actually there are just as many models you can simply meet on the street. They are ordinary in their beauty, natural and unaware of their charm.

These are the people I would like to paint.

Discover more about the artist at his website: www.maciejkempinski.pl

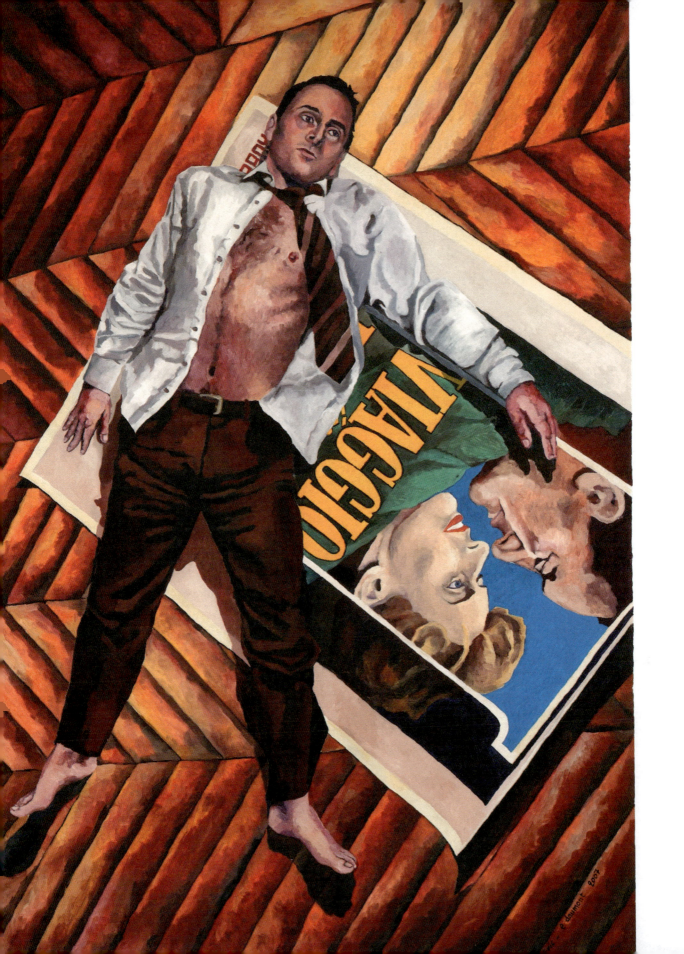

Eric Daumont

Born April 1968 in Paris, Eric Daumont began his studies in classical literature and art and attended the Estienns School of Applied Arts.

In the early 1980s, he traded his 35mm camera for a second hand Roleiflex. He roams the streets of Paris by night in search of bold and daring men. In the late 90's he rediscovered painting and created several series; cinema posters, a sofa series, and a mirror series. The concept of his work is always similar: The nude male offered up to the world.

Art of Man: Why do you focus on the male figure in your portfolio?
Eric Daumont: A painter systematically has a dialogue with his painting, but that doesn't interest me. What interests me is to attempt to fulfill my existence, try and fill a void which haunts me and isolates me. As a cure, I've never found anything better than to meet 'the other,' and as I like sleeping next to men, 'the other' is most often a man.

AOM: What's most unique about your approach?
E.D.: I don't believe that my approach is different than that of other painters, I would say that I'm possibly more obsessive, in effect nothing has turned me away from my quest for 'the other' in 15 years. The stages of my creative process are as follows: the meeting, the photo session, choosing the image, the painting.

The photo session seems to me the most important part. The painting is only the witness, the alibi, the proof of the meeting. It is like a cinema poster, it signals that a meeting has taken place, an exchange, an emotion; something has passed between the object and the eye, *the desired object*. I search and probe always from behind my lens.

I wait behind my camera for 'the other,' the intimate gift, this thing which constitutes all of us. By desire, compulsion, emotion, I try to bring the subject little by little to deliver himself to a form of abandonment. I begin again and again without stopping in the hope of finding and receiving that unique intimate gift. That is how I see my work.

AOM: Have you encountered any issues about having the male figure in your work?
E.D.: Yes, all the time, the male nude stays in the closet; it remains difficult finding a place for it in galleries and with the public in general. Luckily, there is an active gay audience. Thank you to the gay community.

Left: Daumont, *Eric Portrait*, oil, 51 x 74 in. 2007

Above: Daumont, *Mostafa Portrait*, oil, 51 x 74 in. 2011   Right: Daumont, *Yovan Portrait*, oil, 51 x 74 in. 2011

AOM: Do you see a change in the acceptance of the male figure as subject?
E.D.: Things are getting better slowly. The Masculine exhibition/Masculine at the Musée d'Orsay in 2013 was sold out, and things are moving in Paris. The public remains hesitant but is opening up little by little. The male has become an object like the female figure.

What's more, pornography has slowly and quietly become more banal, the new generation tends to be more open minded than their elders, sexuality continues to open up, the quest for happiness is still difficult for us all but the 'leitmotiv' in everyone stays.

Opinions are more and more tolerant. Despite everything, there are always conventional concerns. I avoid depicting the male subject as a sex object. I prefer to look for something more universal in the representation of the male. It's Mr. Normal who moves me and makes me fall in love, it's for him that I always have this deep-seated need to surpass myself in my paintings.

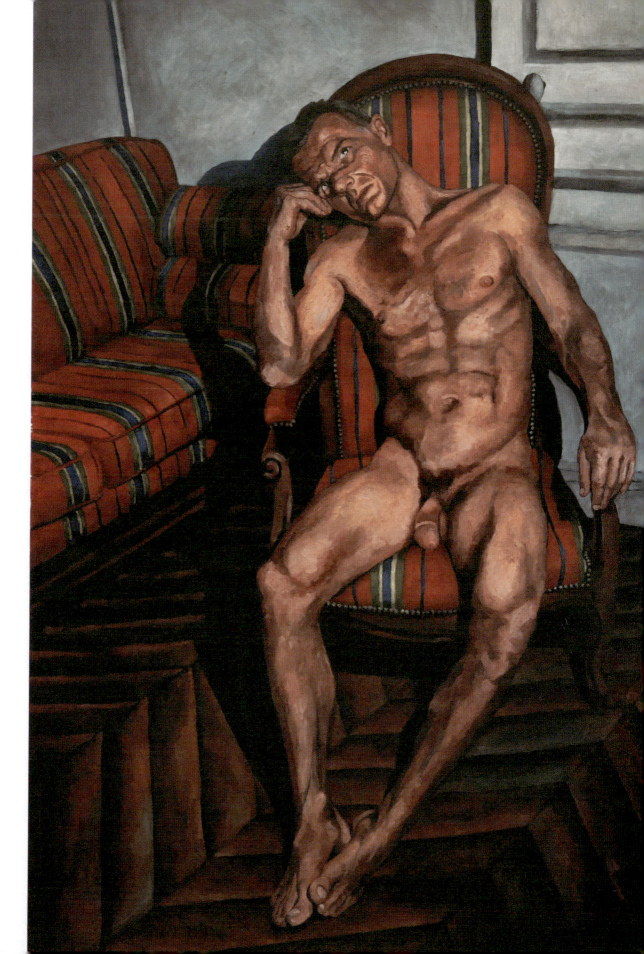

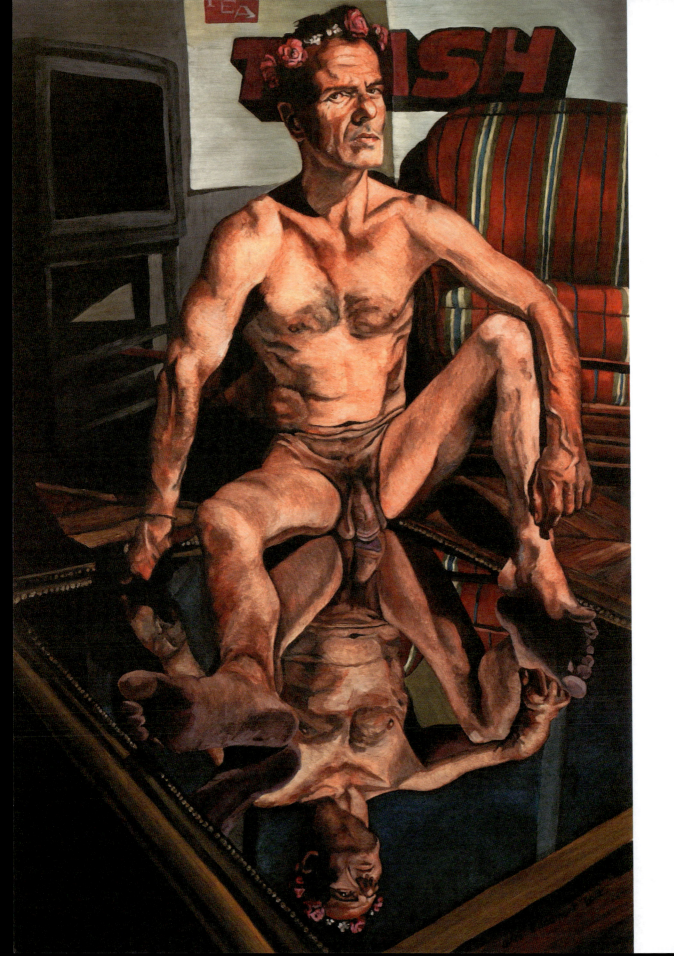

AOM: Where do you get your models?
E.D.: I pester those who are close to me, my colleagues, my friends, to convince them to pose nude for my paintings. It's tiresome for me, for them, but when it works, it's awesome.

On the other hand, a professional model who is paid and undresses before the lens when we don't yet have a relationship together fills me with frustration. In general, I need two or three years in order to "know and appreciate" a professional model fully and be able to finally attempt a painting. When I feel they are close, everything falls into place. I find pleasure in painting them. Emotion drives everything in me, like instinct in animals.

AOM: What's the best or worst thing about having friends model for you?
E.D.: The worst experience is when your friends point to your canvasses and say "I'm begging you, don't do that!" "Be nice to me, hey? Promise, no wrinkles! No large backside, okay? Promise." So you see what they really think, and they are shocked to see themselves painted like a piece of meat, you understand better the extent of your responsibility. Of course I've been tempted to work using photos of strangers but I have no heart for it. In the end it's the stress of what I believe I owe to my model that spurs me on, takes me on to congratulations—or disaster. Luckily, I haven't yet lost a friend because of my paintings.

Daumont, *Yovan Portrait*, oil, 51 x 74 in. 2013

AOM: What direction is your work moving in?
E.D.: I always want to progress, see better, capture better, and produce better. I can see myself painting a single model for a whole year, without letting up. I hope to include more anecdotal elements, small pebbles strewn across a canvas like clues for the observer's pleasure.

AOM: Do you remember the first time you ever sold a work of Art?
E.D.: My first sales are an embarrassment because they were bought by those close to me who wanted to keep their painting. It's awkward because they shouldn't have to pay for something they have generated. My paintings must disappear and live somewhere else.

AOM: When did you first want to be an artist?
E.D.: I don't like the word artist; these days the first idiot to come out of a reality show is an artist, I say get lost! I don't feel like an artist, I want to be a good craftsman, a good painter. To paint is to labor, it's a skill, it's to be tenacious. The whole semantic field on inspiration and artists bore me stiff.

AOM: Do you collect Arts?
E.D.: Yes, old cinema posters.

AOM: Who would you love to model for you?
E.D.: My neighbor, Manuel Valls or Chance Caldwell!

Explore more of the artist's work at: www.ericdaumont.com or contact his gallery via francoisryckelynck@yahoo.fr

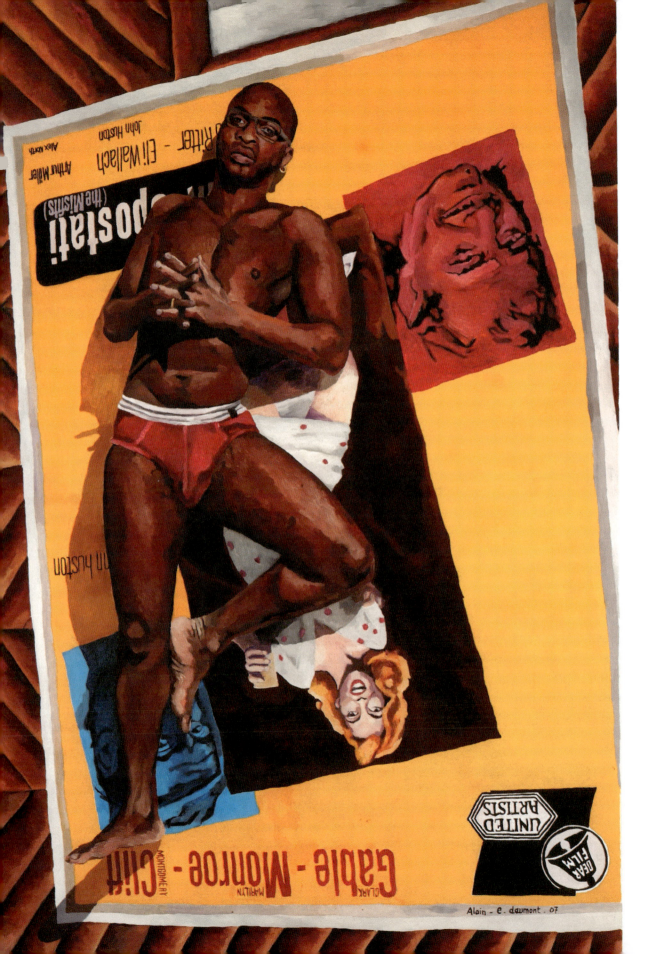

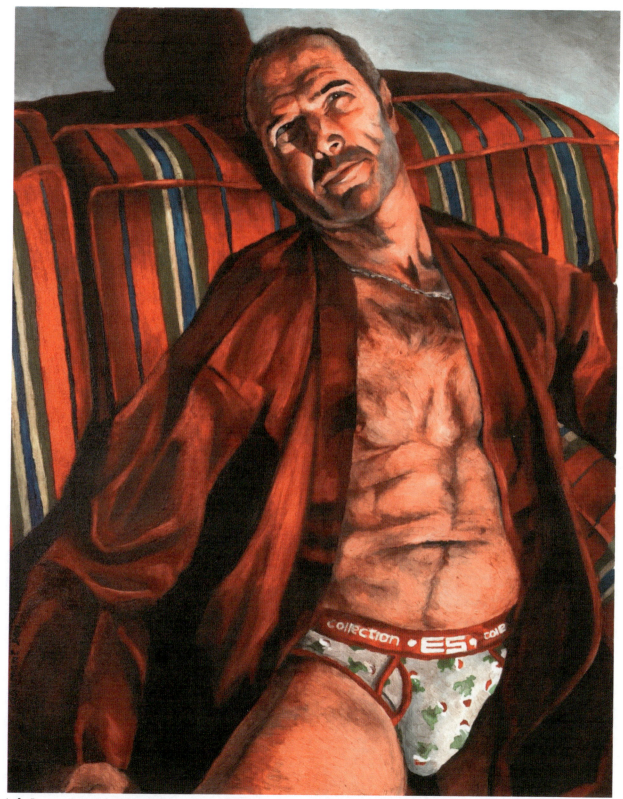

Left: Daumont, *Yannis Portrait*, oil, 51 x 74 in. 2007   Above: Daumont, *Guy Portrait*, oil, 23 x 31 in. 2011

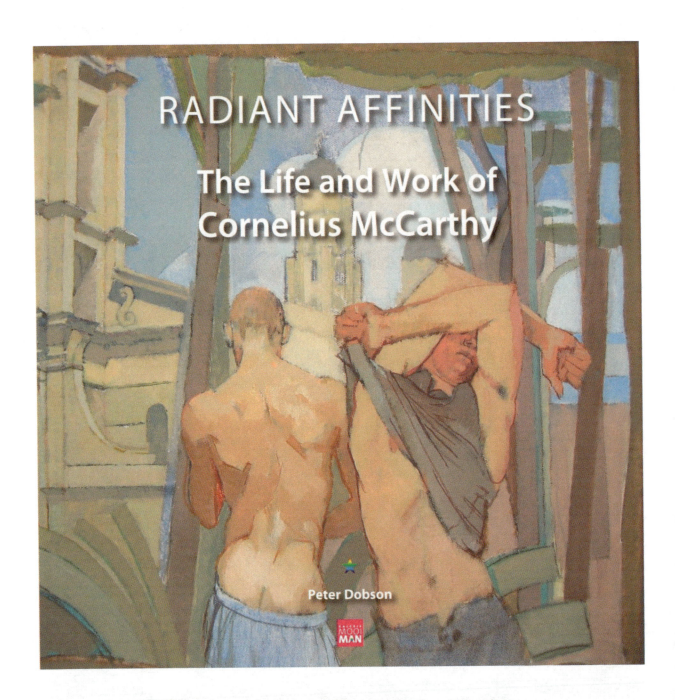

A new book from Mooi Man Gallery. Limited to 500 editions.
For more information please contact:
www.mooi-man.nl or by sending an e-mail to galerie@mooi-man.nl

Featured Artists & Websites

These artists have 50% or more of their portfolios dedicated to the classical male figure and have been featured in *The Art Of Man*.

Manuel A. Acevedo
www.facebook.com/M.A.A.187

Tom Acevedo
www.beguilestudio.com
www.lymaneyerart.com

Robert M Adamcik
www.lymaneyerart.com

Syed Ali Arif
www.facebook.com/artbyarif

Grant Arnold Anderson
www.nondeadartist.com

Aleksander Balos
www.annnathangallery.com
www.redgallerydoor.com

Valentin Bakardjiev
www.vbakardjiev.net

Daniel Barkley
www.danielbarkley.com

Alexei Biryukoff
www.biryukoff.com

Peter Bowles
www.peterbowles.net

Brett Braniff
www.facebook.com/brent.braniff

Francisco Cabas
www.francabas.com

Maciel Cantelmo
www.galleryxo.com

Tony de Carlo
www.tonydecarlo.com

William Cash
www.lymaneyerart.com

Jean Chaîney
www.jean-chainey.com

Gary Chapman
www.garychapmanart.com

James Childs
www.jameschilds.com

Peter Churcher
www.peterchurcher.com.au

Richard Claraval
www.richardclaraval.com

Tyrus Clutter
www.tyrusclutter.com

Steve Cronkite
www.lymaneyerart.com

Anthony Cudahy
www.anthonycudahy.com

Remko van Drongelen
www.remkovandrongelen.com

Tom Durham
www.tomduramsculpture.com

William Eicholtz
www.dishboydreaming.com

DebiLynn Fendley
debilynnfendleystudios.artspan.com

Dominic Finocchio
www.dominicfinocchio.com

Robert Fontanelli
www.robertfontanelli.com

Jacob Fossum
www.JacobFossum.com

Rita Foster
www.ritafoster.blogspot.com

Christian Gaillard
www.christiangaillard.com

Bob Gherardi
www.Gherardi.com

E. Gibbons
www.lymaneyerart.com

Jakub Godziszewski
jakubgodziszewski.daportfolio.com

Ron Griswold
www.rongriswold.com

Rick Herold
www.Rickherold.com

Cauro Hige
cauro.web.fc2.com

Philip Hitchcock
www.philiphitchcock.com

Bonnie Hofkin
www.hofkin.com

Mark Horst
www.markhorststudio.com

Sabin Howard
www.sabinhoward.com

Julian Hsiung
www.julianhsiung.com

Gerard Huber
www.GerardHuber.com
Lizardi Harp Gallery, CA

Francisco Hurtz
franciscohurtz.tumblr.com

Eric Itschert
eric-itschert-painter.skynetblogs.be

Hideki Koh
www.JapaneseGayArt.com

Len Leone
www.lenleone.com

Douglas Malone
www.douglasmalone.com

Ryan Martin
www.ryanstevenmartin.com

Alan McGowan
www.alanmcgowan.com

James Messana
www.jamesmessana.com

Joshua Meyer
www.joshua-meyer.com

Jordan Mejias
www.jordanmejias.com

Musk Ming
www.muskming.com

Evan Morse
www.lymaneyerart.com

James Mortimer
www.jamesfreemangallery.com

Tom Muscatello
muscmanart.blogspot.com

Lyubomir Naydenov
www.lyubomir-naydenov.com

Ward Nipper
www.wardnipperdrawings.com

Mel Odom
www.melodomart.com

Andrew Ogus
andrew-ogus.artistwebsites.com

Gonzalo Orquín
www.gonzalo-orquin.com

Derek Overfield
www.derekoverfield.com

Eustace Palladion
stathispalladino.blogspot.co.uk

Jose Parra
www.joseparra.com

Keith Perelli
flickr.com/photos/perelli

Miriam Perez
www.miriamperez.com.mx

Kevin E. Peterson
www.kepart.com
www.lymaneyerart.com

Barahona Possollo
www.barahonapossollo.com

David Powers
www.davidcpowers.com

Dan Pyle
www.danpyleartist.com

Fran Recacha
www.franrecacha.com

Wade Reynolds
Lizardi/Harp Gallery, CA
626-791-8123

Robert Richards
RobertWRichards@earthlink.net
www.tinyurl.com/3vbsjcj

Paul Richmond
www.paulrichmondstudio.com
www.lymaneyerart.com

R. E. Roberts
www.rer.name

Paul Rybarczyk
www.artworkbypaul.com

Carmine Santaniello
www.tinyurl.com/8y9lbsc

Martin-Jan van Santen
www.martinjanvansanten.com

Ivor Sexton
www.bespokeartgallery.com

Miriam Schulman
www.schulmanArt.com

Philip Shadbolt
www.philipshadbolt.co.uk

Robert Sherer
www.robertsherer.com
www.lymaneyerart.com

Kenya Shimizu
www.JapaneseGayArt.com

Esther Simmonds-MacAdam
www.esthersm.com

Christopher Sousa
christophersousa.tumblr.com

Sergey Sovkov
artnow.ru/ru/gallery/3/1558.html

Richard Stabbert
www.rstabbert.com

Sergei Svetlakov
www.sergeisvetlakov.com

John Tarantola's
Johntarantola.blogspot.com

Naoki Tatsuya
www.JapaneseGayArt.com

George Towne
www.georgetowneart.com

Robert F. Varga
robertvargapaintings.com

Rebecca Venn
www.rebeccavenn.com

Joseph Vorgity
www.josephvorgity.com

Richard Vyse
manartbyvyse.blogspot.com

Steve Walker (d-2012)
www.lymaneyerart.com

Richard Wallace
www.richardwallace.org

Patrick Webb
www.Patrick-webb.com

Carolyn Weltman
www.carolynweltman.com

Todd Yeager
www.yeagermuseum.com

Yujiro
www.JapaneseGayArt.com

Recommended Galleries

Lyman-Eyer Gallery
Online
www. lymaneyerart.com

Leslie/Lohman Gay Art Museum
Manhattan, NY
www.leslielohman.org

Firehouse Gallery
Bordentown, NJ
www.firehousegallery.com/info.htm

PHD Gallery
St. Louis, MO
www.phdstl.com

Lizardi/Harp Gallery
Pasadena CA
626-791-8123

Galerie Mooi-Man
Groningen, Netherlands
www.mooi-man.NL

Alexander Salazar Fine Art
San Diego, CA
www.alexandersalazarfineart.com

Mayumi International
Japan/Australia
www.JapaneseGayArt.com

Vitruvian Gallery
Washington, DC
www.vitruviangallery.com

Gallery XO
Wilton Manors, FL
www.galleryxo.com

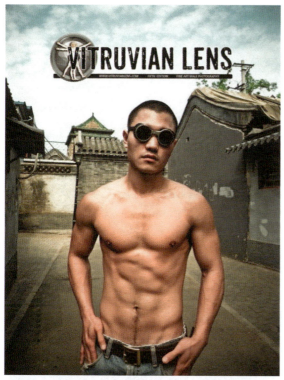

www.VitruvianLens.com

Vitruvian Lens showcases photographers with a fine art approach to the male figure in art.

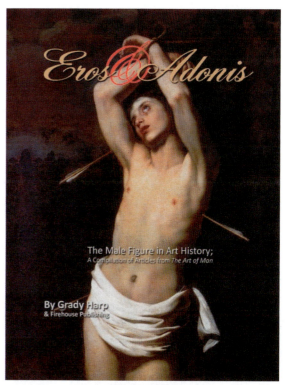

www.TheArtOfMan.net

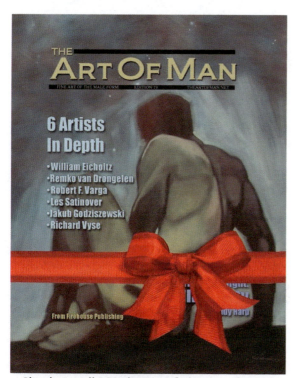

Check out all 20 editions of The Art of Man!
www.TheArtOfMan.net

Eros & Adonis is a collection of art history articles first appearing in *The Art of Man*, issues one through twelve. This compilation focuses on classical fine art of the male figure from the ancient Greeks to artists of the twentieth century. Though today, figurative art is often dominated by the female form, digital imagery, and photography, but it was not always this way, and the evidence is here in this comprehensive collection.

The volume begins with an Introduction by Grady Harp, and contains articles on Jean-Hippolyte Flandrin, Willian-Adolphe Bouguereau, Jean-Léon Gérôme, Thomas Eakins, Jacques-Louis David, Guido Reni, Cornelius McCarthy, Agnolo Bronzino, Icarus, Shozo Nagano, The Orient and the Occident, Greek and Roman Sculpture, Ganymede, Wade Reynolds, The Influence of Saint Sebastian, The Influence of Apollo, William Blake, The Influence of Hercules, and Eugène Frederik Jansson.

Recommended Websites

FirehousePublications.com

TheArtOfMan.net

PowerfullyBeautiful.com

100ArtistsBook.com

100ArtistsBook.tumblr.com

www.sachetmixte.com

www.VitruvianLens.com

www.hellomrmag.com

Books from Michael hone:
www.amazon.com/author/mbhone

Other Books We Publish

Powerfully Beautiful
www.createspace.com/3382894

365 Art Quotes
www.createspace.com/3904538

100 Artists of the Male Figure
www.100ArtistsBook.com

Provincetown Memories [Full Color]
www.createspace.com/4504319

Provincetown Memories [Black & White]
www.createspace.com/4512557

Vitruvian Lens
www.VitruvianLens.com

More info about The Art of Man, , back issues, submissions, and more can be found at: www.theartofman.net

Please Note: No assumptions should be made about the artists included in this book; their gender or sexuality. Though all of the artists dedicate a significant portion of their portfolio to the classical male form, they are equally adept in painting, drawing, and sculpting many other subjects as well. We always seek artists who dedicate 50% or more of their portfolio to the male figure and promote those artists at no cost here. More information about being featured in a future edition can be found on our website:

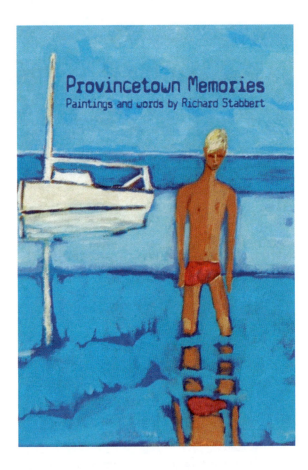

This is the full color artist's edition: Richard Stabbert is a self-taught painter. He documents the people in his life, both past and present, referencing them, the objects around him, and his love of the beach. All of his images are tied together by a sensuality of brushstroke. He limits his palette to evoke spare, almost graphic forms, as color in itself and line that have a resonance and symbolism for Stabbert.

Picasso once said, *"It took me four years to paint like Raphael, but a lifetime to paint like a child."*

Stabbert is one who embraces the simplicity of his style and approaches his work with passion and enthusiasm. We see his words and works through the eyes of adolescent self-discovery and passion. Richard describes young love, from first flirt to first love, and everything in-between, most often centered here, in the artist colony of Provincetown, Massachusetts. The Newest collection from the publishers of *The Art of Man*.

www.createspace.com/4504319

Made in the USA
Lexington, KY
04 September 2015